Patterns One

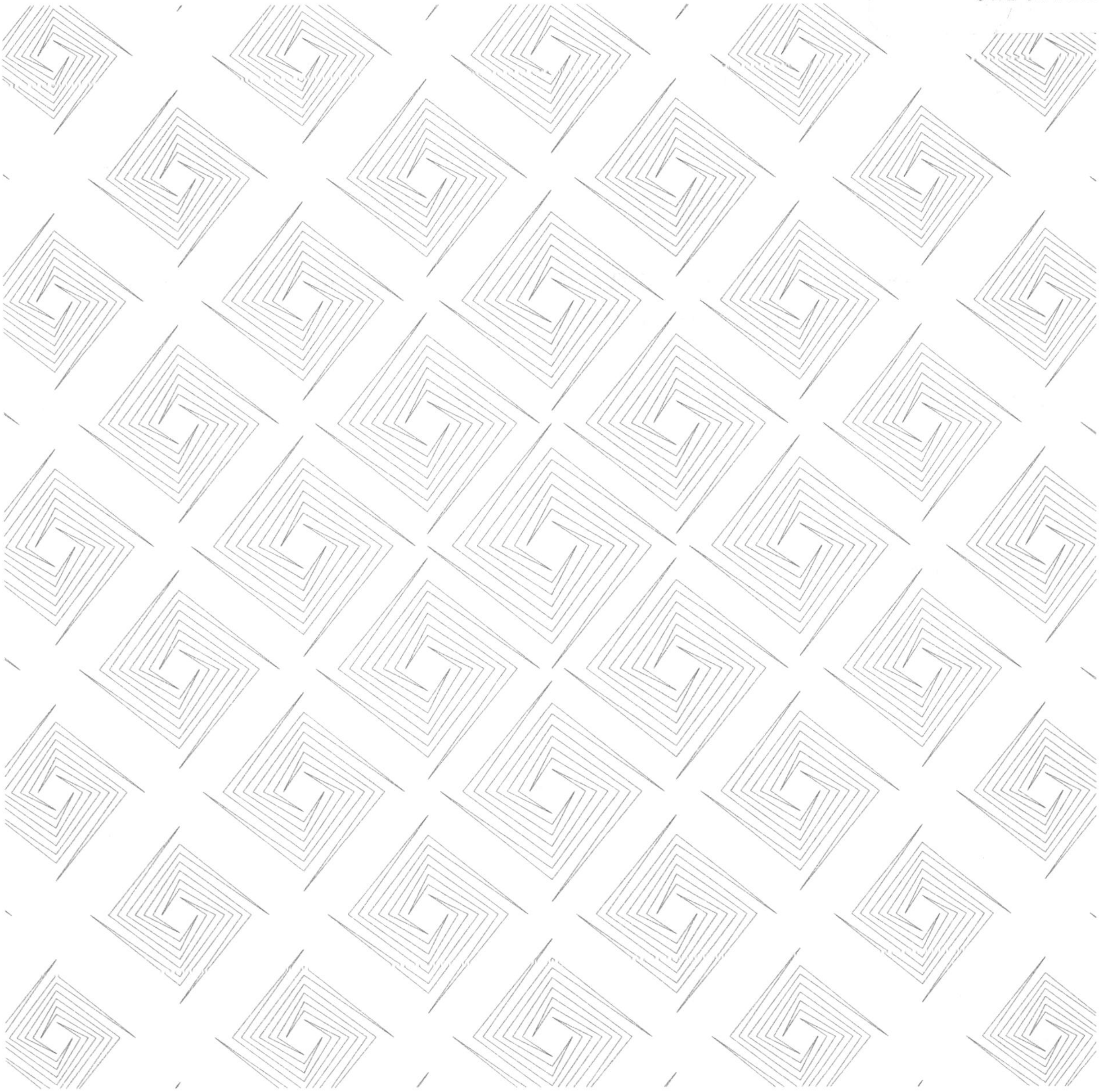

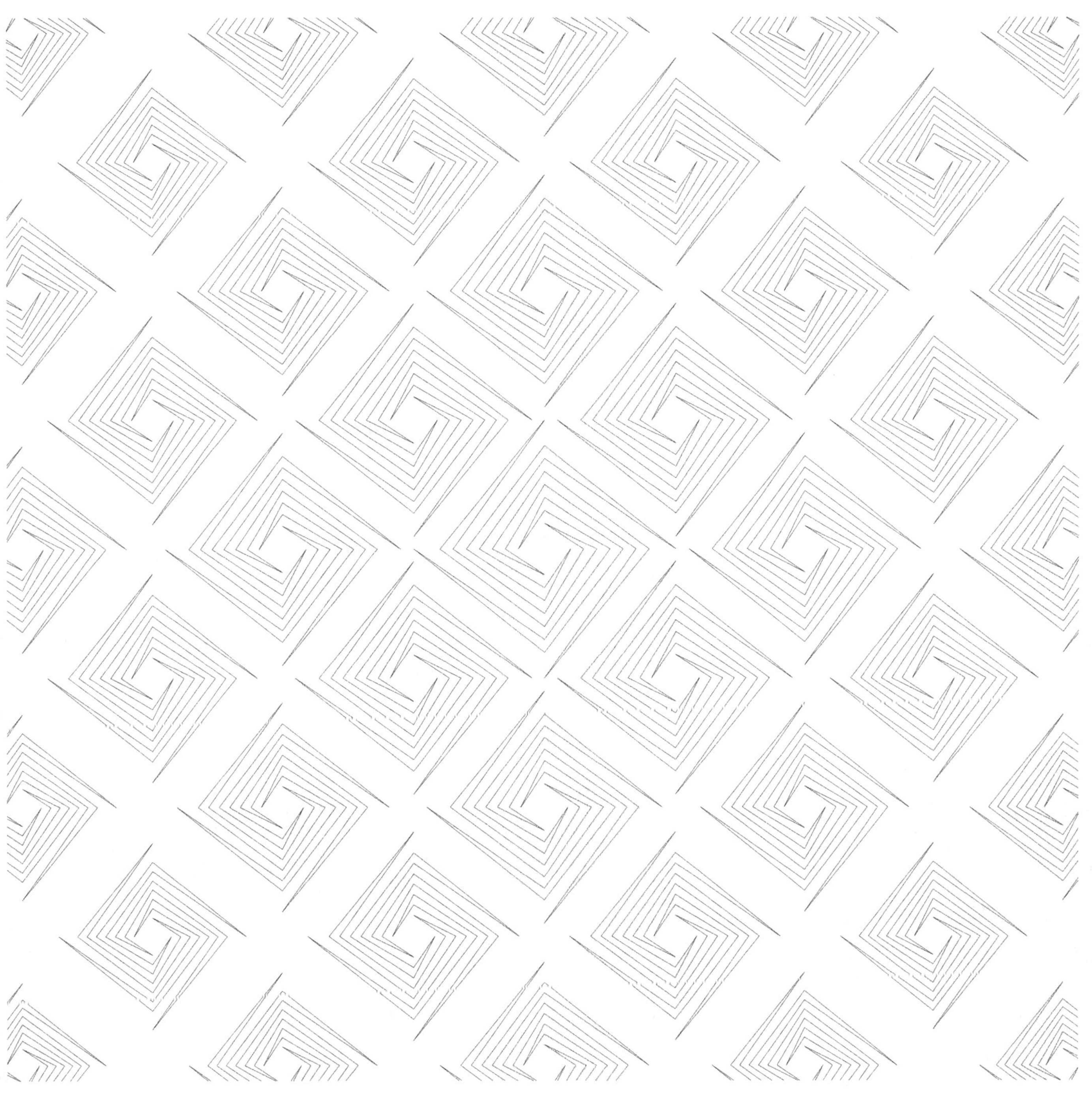

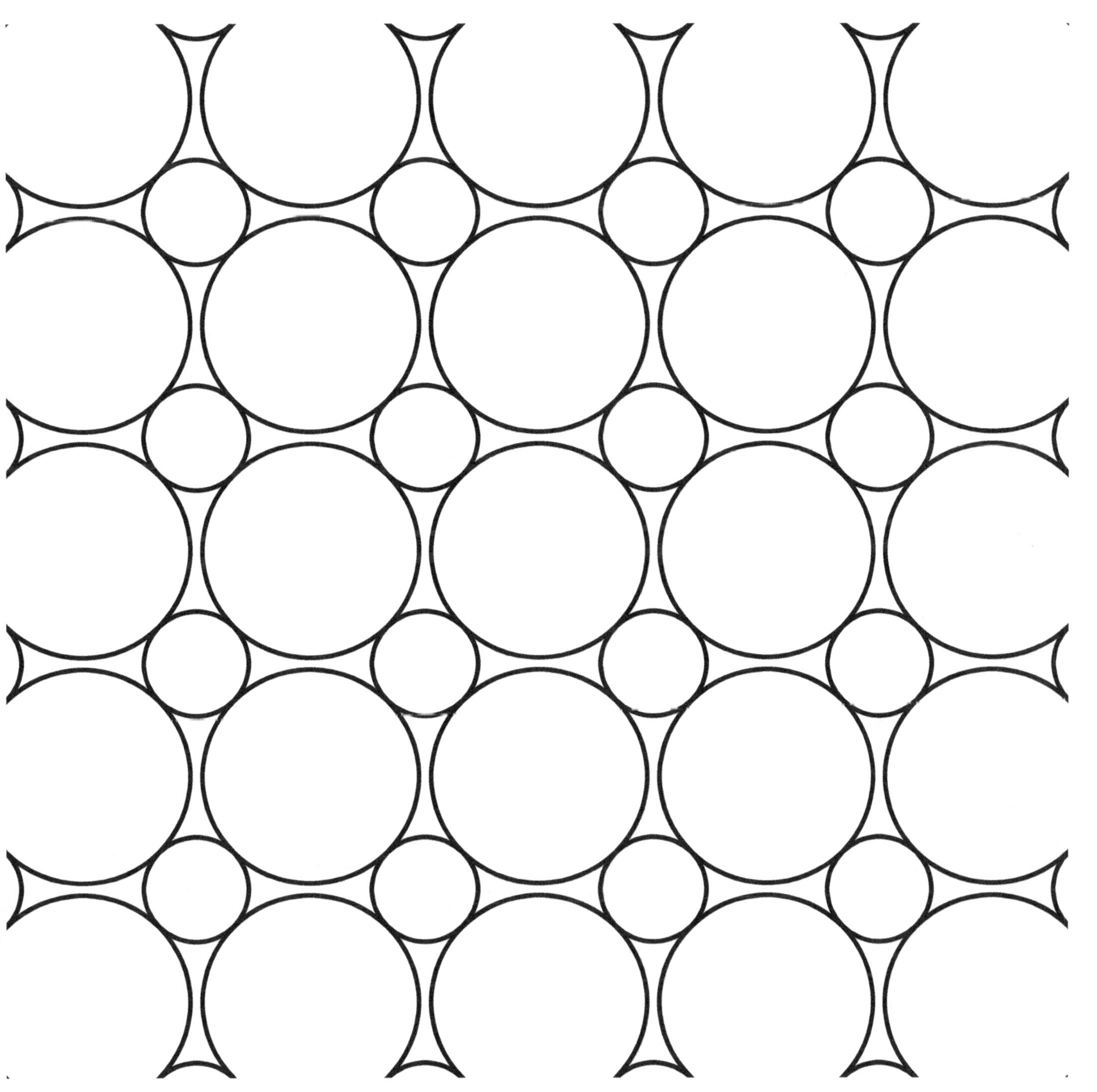

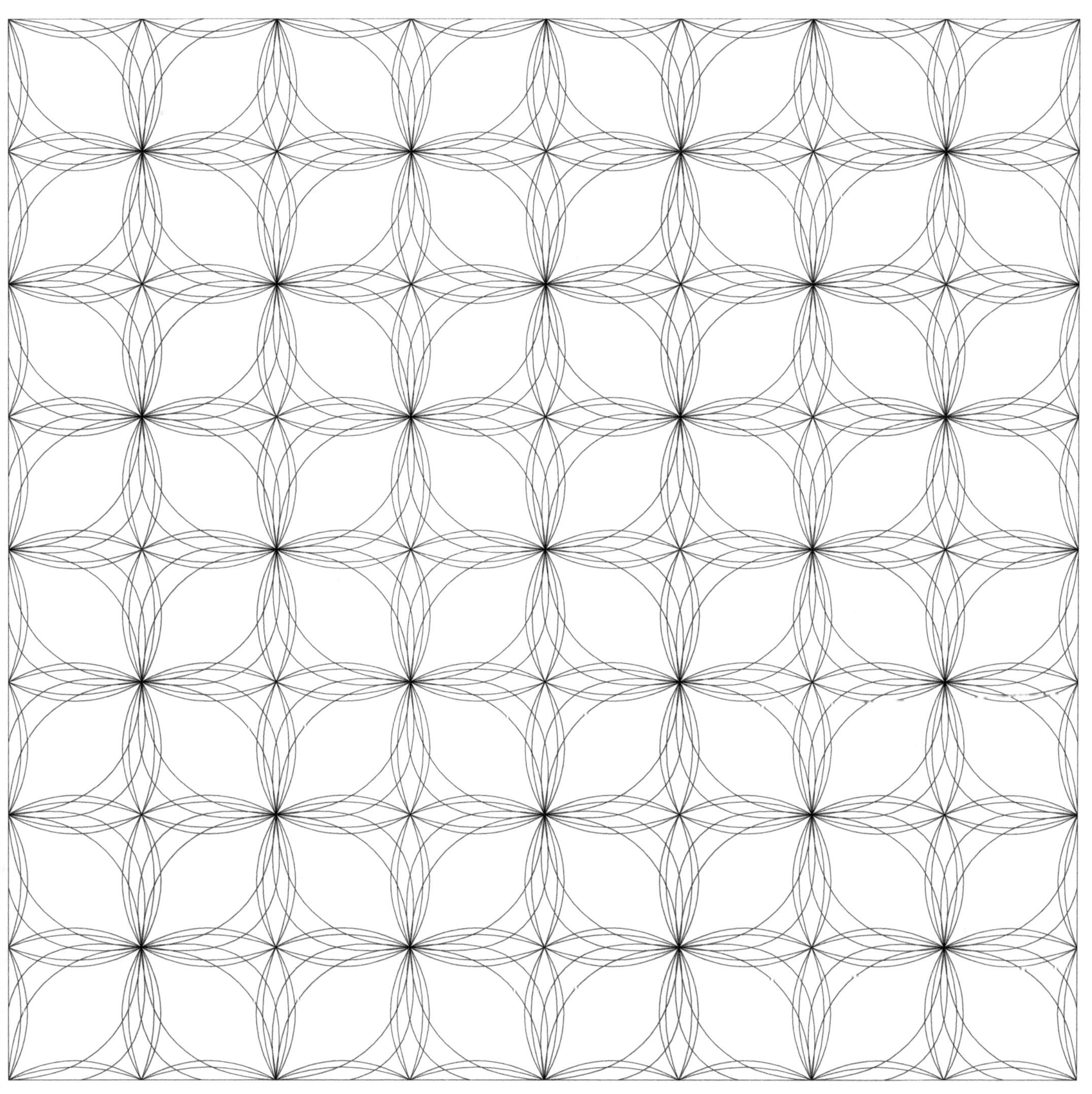

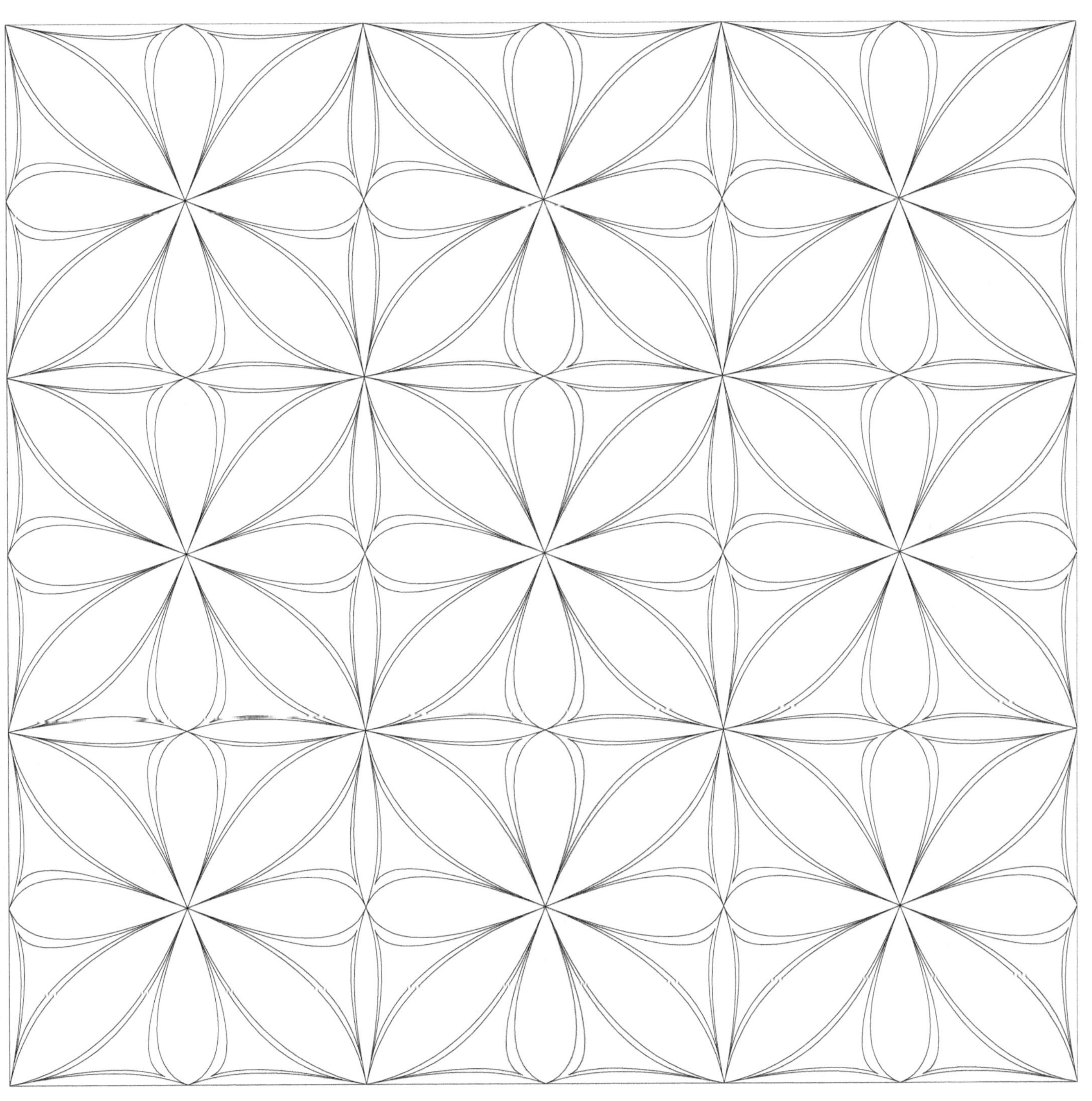

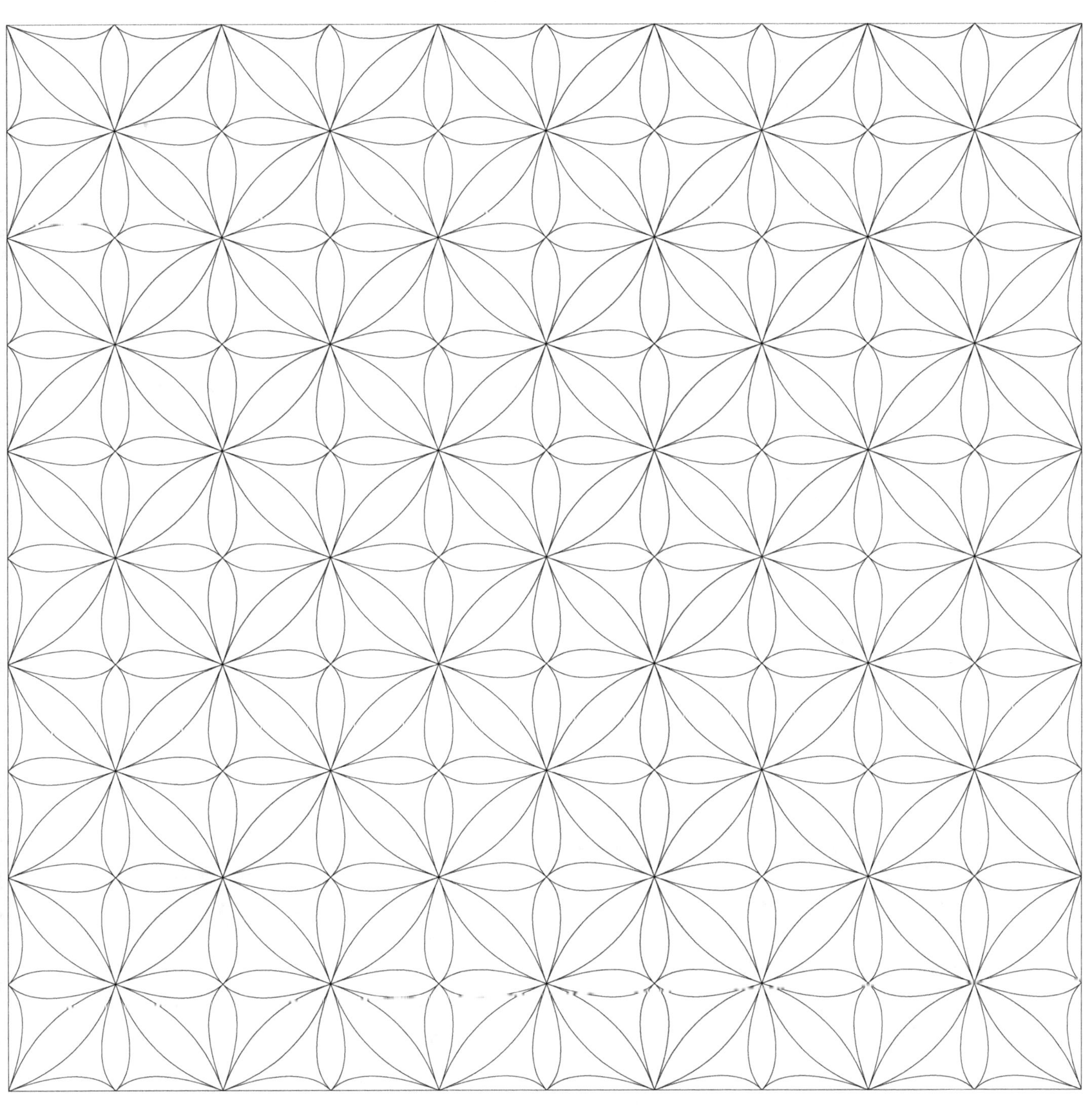

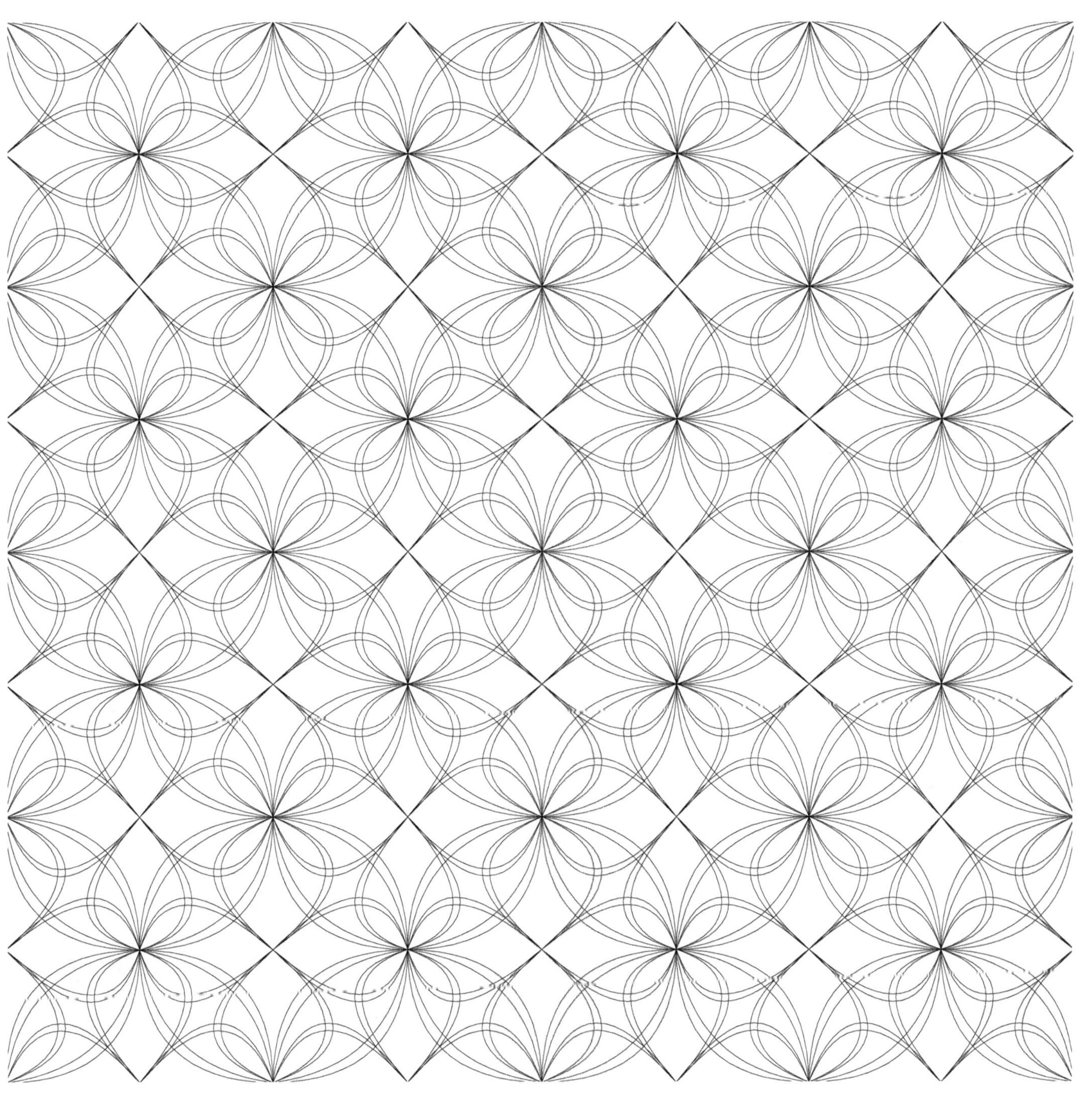

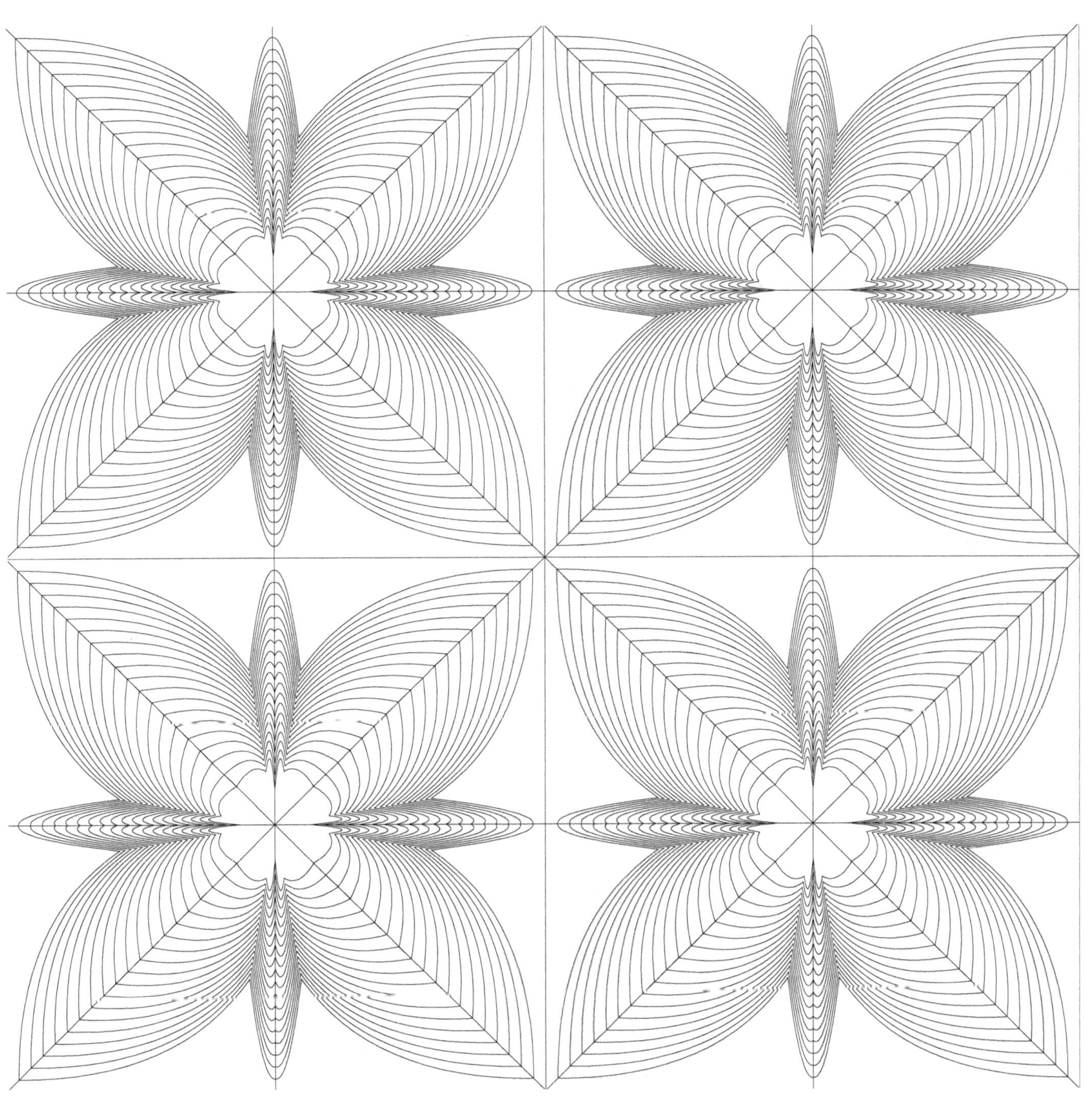

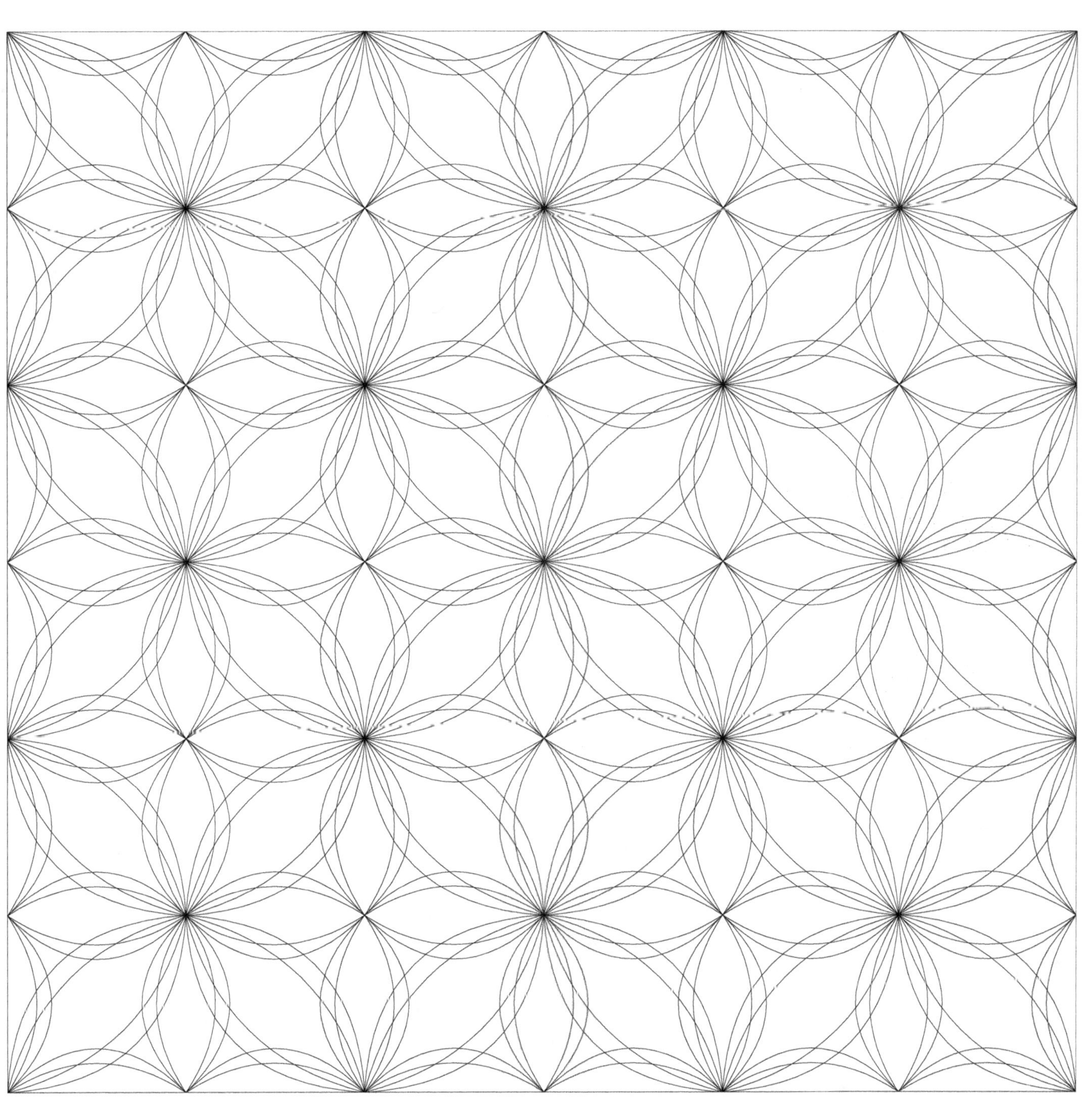

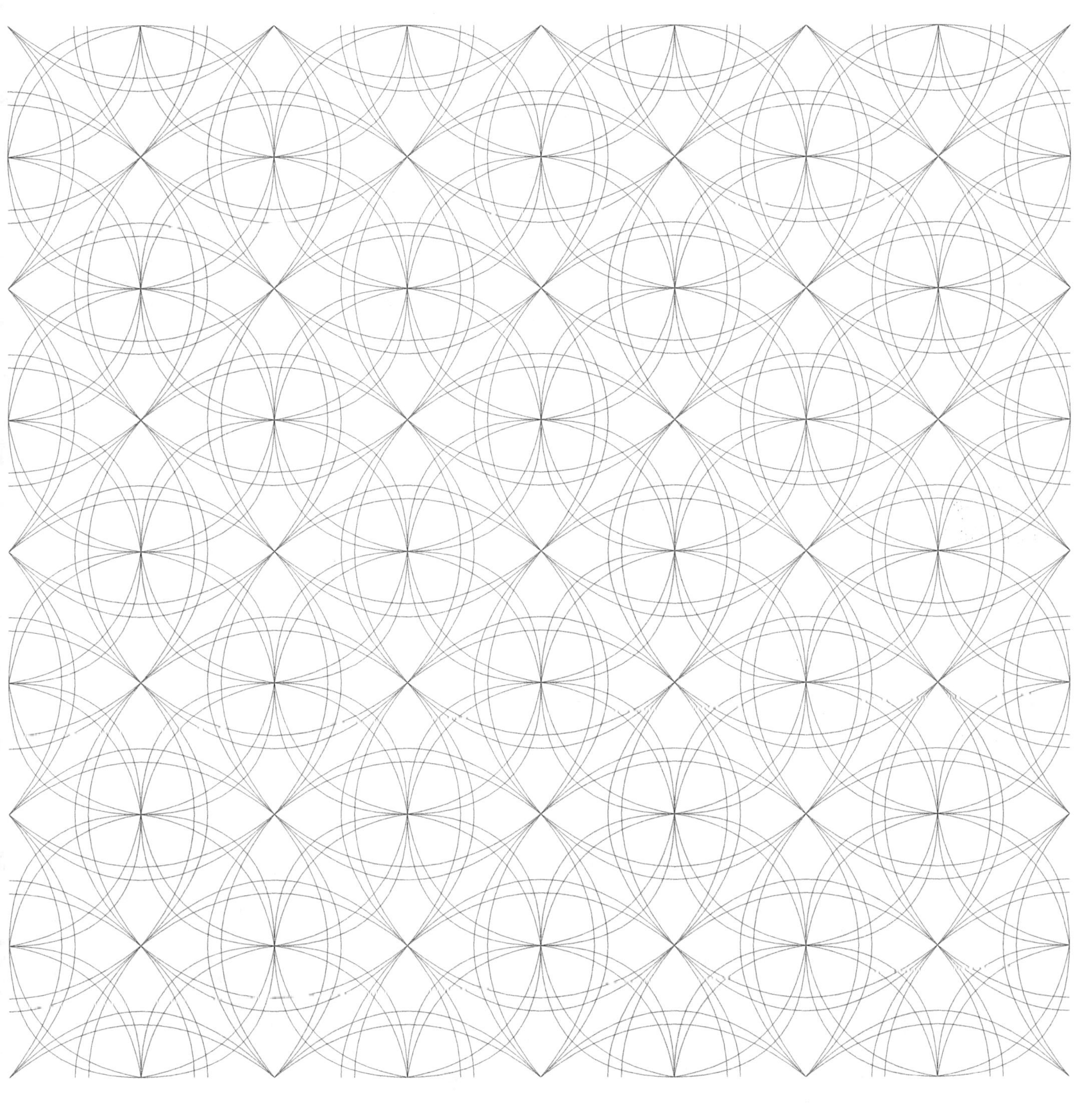

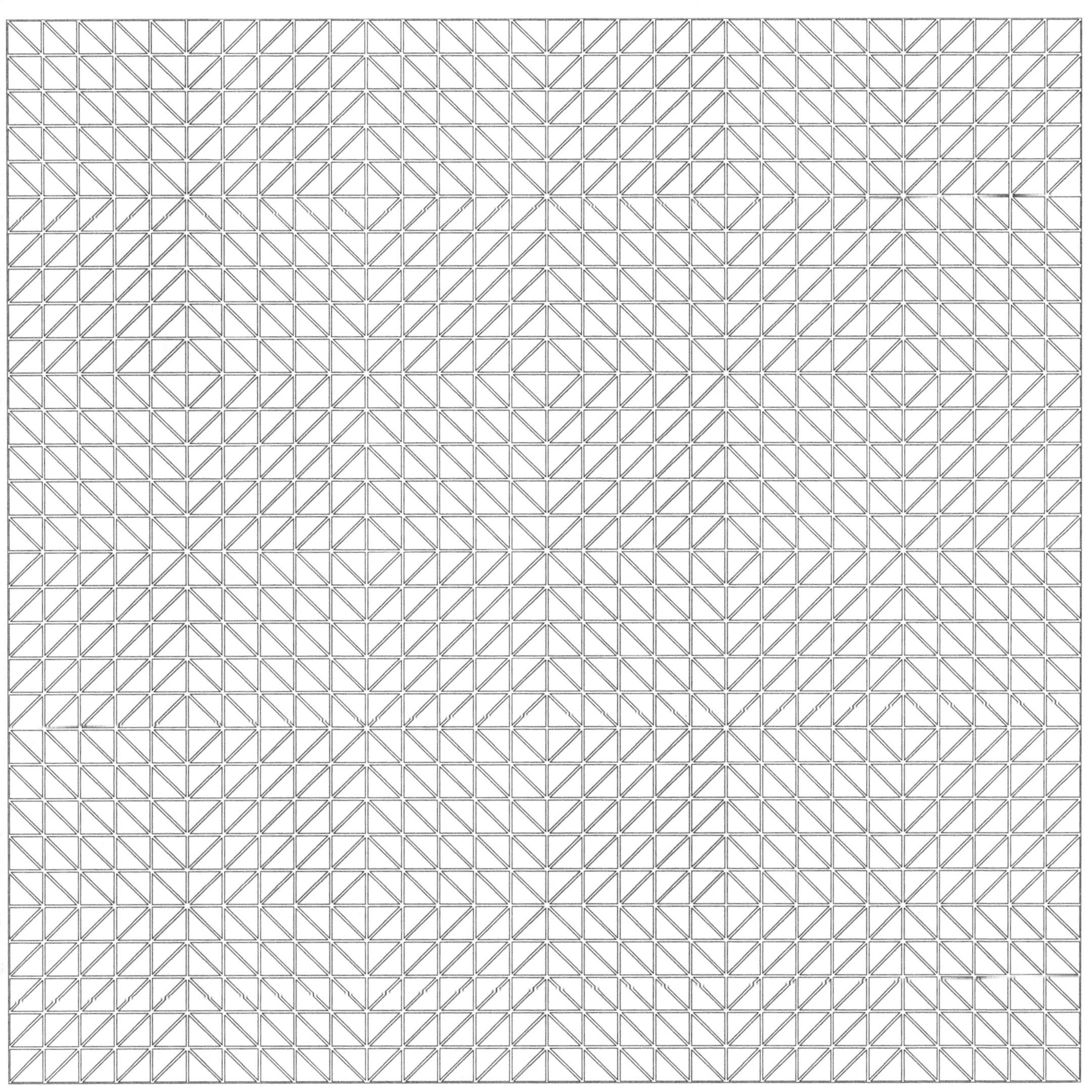